Awakenings

Epiphanies Along a Spiritual Journey

Big Meach

ACKNOWLEDGEMENTS

This project would not be possible without the love, support, and encouragement from those whom I cherish and from those who have stood by me through every step along this part of my journey.

Without my connection and dedication to The Infinite Creator, I would have, do, and be nothing! It is through this identity that I UNDERstand, OVERstand, and INNERstand who I am and what I am to be....I am to be the eyes, hands, feet, and body of The Infinite so that miracles, knowledge, and education can flow and be received.

Thank you to Unity Fellowship Church Movement for introducing me to the practice and acceptance of spiritual critical thinking. This thinking allows me to pierce through all of the dogma and doctrine that binds us to complacency and religiosity. Thank you for assisting me in sharpening my spiritual tools so that I can stand on what I KNOW the INFINITE TO BE!

Thank you Elder Claude Everret Bowen and Rev. Darren McCarroll Jones a.k.a. Muata for teaching me how to go outside the realm of superficiality and mundaneness and for allowing authenticity to reign supreme in my life. Thank you for showing me by example that THE INFINITE speaks to each of us and that no voice is to be silenced or quieted simply because the masses don't agree. Thank you for showing me that is it STILL COOL to be HUMAN along this journey and that The Diety of Religiosity is only a manmade concept that has nothing to do with spiritual growth and/or integrity. Thank you for showing me that each facet of my living is, was, and continues to be REQUIRED for my development into my AUTHENTIC SELF.

To my family - you already know that everything I do is for the betterment of US! We are on our way to building our ESTATE so that the babies will carry on the legacy!

A special thank you goes out to my bffs: "Ole Becka" Eubie Sweet, Joynal Muthleb III, Peter Jackson, Otis Randolf, Ms. Michiee 'Lil Meech' DeVale and my NFL, R.S. Jeffrey. You all have been very instrumental in this leg of the journey by challenging me to stick to my guns and by pushing me forward so that I can propel into greatness...that divine greatness that is already ordained for me, but I sometimes forget how I am connected to it. Thank you for believing in the vision and for never stopping me from seeing it!

An extra special shout out goes to La Troupe des Arts! We've vowed to make sure we show up and TAKE CARE OF BUSINESS!! State, Relate, Prove, and

Conclude...thank you for nearly 30 years of LOVE
and SUPPORT!!

This project is dedicated to all those who are seeking
to find themselves and their spiritual truth. In the
memory of all those who have passed on, have
become an ancestor of this life experience, and have
not been afforded the opportunity to experience life as
I am, I thank you for being the light along this
journey. It is my praise report that you continue to be
the light for others seeking their own epiphanies.

Table of Contents

Awakening The Omniverse

Awakening My Spirit

Awakening My Humanity

Awakening To Me

AWAKENING:

THE OMNIVERSE

I Can NOT Give You LIFE NOR Can I LIVE IT for You!!

Today is another day of reflection for me as I sit and ponder over my life and really LOOK at what I have accomplished and what I want to achieve. I reflected on an area of my life where I wasted a lot of time foolishly and needlessly because I thought I was doing the right thing when I know now that it was not.

I used the slogan 'I have to live for the both of us' whenever I was with people who did not want to participate in what I wanted to do, for people who were sick and shut in, or whenever I thought I was 'teaching them how to live their lives'. I had become so accustomed to giving people everything, and my giving was the result of them NOT living. Because I GAVE them their Life, they did not LIVE their LIVES!!! I WAS LIVING THEIR LIVES FOR THEM!!!

You see, society has taken the scripture 'it's better to give than to receive' to a whole new adulterated level where NOBODY wants to be the giver; EVERYBODY wants to be the receiver. We have redefined the word 'Giver' and made it synonymous with the word 'HANDOUT' - in essence we have allowed people the opportunity to build themselves up to be pimps!!!

The Merriam-Webster Collegiate Dictionary defines the word PIMP as "To make use of, often dishonorably, for one's own gain or benefit" or "A man who solicits for a prostitute, LIVES off HER EARNINGS, and often LIVES OFF HER".

We have taken that whole 'bitch better have my money' mentality and created it as a mantra in every aspect of our lives.

We pimp our parents for their LOVE and UNDERSTANDING because we will not get out into the world and HONOR them by demonstrating and utilizing the gifts, talents, and teaching they have bestowed upon us. INSTEAD, many have decided to stay home and leech our parents dry, EXPECTING them to continue to GIVE us everything.

WE pimp our teachers for their KNOWLEDGE and EDUCATION because we will not do the work to show ourselves approved. We INSTEAD fault the teachers because we will not apply ourselves, take the tests, and do what's needed to matriculate, EXPECTING the teachers to pass us to the next grade levels.

WE pimp our preachers for their SALVATION because we won't study the scriptures and build a relationship with the CREATOR for ourselves. INSTEAD, we hang on to every word of the preacher as if he is a deity, forgetting that the preacher is human like the rest of us with flaws and faults. We EXPECT the preacher to tell us who The CREATOR is, what decisions to make, how to live our lives, and and how to love the CREATOR – we never challenge the preacher's interpretations or seek answers that align with our individual journeys.

We pimp our communities for CHARITY because we continuously run to them for handouts and freebies without restoring the supply or volunteering to assist with others who are in need. INSTEAD we gripe and complain because the centers don't have enough resources and we EXPECT the community to always be ready to GIVE us EVERYTHING without us working toward keeping the surplus plentiful.

We pimp our spouses/significant others for their SUPPORT and COMPANIONSHIP because we CONNED them into believing we were the person sent by God to be their life partner. INSTEAD we were looking for someone else to foot the responsibility of 'paying the cost to be the boss'; EXPECTING them to relinquish the benefits from all the hard work and responsibility over to them without question or pause!!!!

Today's world has become a LAZY world. We have become complacent with allowing folks to sit back and DO NOTHING, they expect someone else to do it for them. I am one who must admit to assisting the world in turning folks into 'Spiritual Welfare Recipients'. Just like those who use the system as a means of survival and not as a stepping stone, we have the AUDACITY to get upset, attitudinal, and bent out of shape whenever someone does not GIVE us anything and EXPECTS us to work for it!!!!

I CAN NOT GIVE YOU LIFE NOR CAN I LIVE IT FOR YOU!!!

The time has come for us to get a grip and LEARN that this PIMPING/WELFARE system does not work!!! The Quality of Life for people is in peril; it's up to US individually to decide what kind of life we want for ourselves and to GIVE that kind of life to OURSELVES!!! You see, here's one scripture that most of our pimps have forgotten about: If a man/woman don't work, he/she don't eat!!!

What contributions are YOU bringing to the table of life? What skills and talents are you blessed with that can sustain YOU? How are YOU putting the pieces of YOUR puzzle together for YOUR life? How are YOU participating in YOUR LIFE to make YOUR LIFE WORK FOR YOU?

Once we answer these questions for ourselves, we can then begin the process of LIVING our LIVES! Living is an action word...it's doing, it's participating in making and producing those things which bring forth happiness and JOY. To live life is to grow and nurture our senses. It's to experience new things and create new avenues for our senses to be challenged and grow. Living life is to become enriched in culture and to create a culture for others to enjoy. It's to understand that each person has a story to share and a world to create for others to enjoy and to experience. Living life is to embrace change and newness and to understand your individual likes and dislikes so that you can surround yourself with those things that bring you JOY and that encourage and stimulate growth.

I CAN NOT GIVE YOU LIFE NOR CAN I LIVE IT FOR YOU!!!

The Creator has given us the BREATH of LIFE and it's up to us LIVE!!! In other words, here is the 'T': The CREATOR IS NOT GOING TO and WILL NOT LIVE LIFE FOR US, so why do we EXPECT anyone else to LIVE FOR US?

It's time for us to HONOR ourselves by coming out of the shadows of pimpdom and spiritual welfare and RESPECT what The CREATOR supplied as the world's gift: YOU and YOUR LIFE!!!

Honor and Respect your gifts
Honor and Respect your talents
Honor and Respect your creativity
Honor and Respect your world
Honor and Respect your parents
Honor and Respect your community
Honor and Respect your teachers
Honor and Respect your preachers
Honor and Respect your CREATOR

We achieve this by HONORING and RESPECTING our individuality and our LIVES by doing those things which brings us ABSOLUTE JOY!!! GIVE yourself the LIFE you WANT and LIVE YOUR LIFE to its fullest!!!

I Shall not and Will not Be Denied!!

I dedicate this passage to all those who are struggling with BECOMING what they want, BELIEVING that they deserve to have it, and those who are BASKING in the promises of the Almighty.

For far too long, we have allowed ourselves to believe that desiring things which are considered to be 'the finer things in life' are only for those who have the resources, opportunities, connections, and good fortune to achieve and attain them. We have allowed ourselves to live in a space where the belief system relies on the majority of the population to accept the idea that mediocrity is the highest level of success that one can aspire to achieve. We have allowed ourselves to sustain in the consciousness that stagnation and degradation is to be the dominant motivator of our culture.

Well it is now time for our culture, our population, humankind, and the world to shake the Neanderthal nonsense and treacherous thoughts loose and begin walking UPRIGHT in the wisdom and the understanding of our conscious power and believe the proclamation:

I SHALL NOT and WILL NOT BE DENIED!!!

As entities, representatives, examples, ambassadors, and definitive echoes of the Almighty Creator, it is up to US to live up to our birthright!!! It is up to US to utilize the gifts and talents which have been bestowed upon us at our inception. It is up to US to MAKE and BE the Culture, Population, Humankind, and World we want! It is up to us to STAND and continuously, boldly, and FERVENTLY PROCLAIM...

I SHALL NOT and WILL NOT BE DENIED!!!

I SHALL NOT and WILL NOT BE DENIED access to living a wonderful, spirit-filled life simply because others do not understand MY relationship with the Creator.

I SHALL NOT and WILL NOT BE DENIED access to having loving, fulfilling relationships in my life simply because others do not comprehend the depths of how I share and need to receive LOVE in all its forms: Agape (unconditional love of, for, and by God), Eros (passionate, romantic, and sexual love), Philia (natural, virtuous love for family and friends), and Xenia (hospitality, gratitude love)!!!

I SHALL NOT and WILL NOT BE DENIED access to building my personal wealth and my estate simply because others do not exercise the essence of 'The Golden Rule' or because others want to comprehend why my existence is just as important as theirs.

I SHALL NOT and WILL NOT BE DENIED access to enriching my life through matriculation and my educational endeavors simply because others view my ideas and contributions to this side of creation as unconventional, controversial, or unorthodox.

I SHALL NOT and WILL NOT BE DENIED access to the benefits of great comprehensive health, whether it be mentally, spiritually, emotionally, and physically, simply because others have demonstrated and displayed efforts of annihilation, genocide, and destruction toward the population and sections thereof.

I SHALL NOT and WILL NOT BE DENIED access to all of the promises the Creator has already ordained for me simply because of others' perceptions and concepts of how I should live MY life.

It is a beautiful thing to come into one's own SELF!!! Once one discovers that TRUE POWER exists when the TRUE SELF is recognized and UNCOVERED, the UNIVERSE supplies the platform for one to STAND and CONTINUOUSLY, BOLDLY, and FERVENTLY PROCLAIM…

I SHALL NOT and WILL NOT BE DENIED!!!

Claim your Existence, Walk in your Inheritance, Speak with Authority, and Accept nothing LESS THAN THE BEST!!!

Be blessed and know that YOU are the GREATEST GIFT of LIFE!

Let NO ONE Put Asunder

Welcome in, oh Precious Sweet Spirit, as I bask in your presence and your love thanking the Master Creator for yet another glorious day! A' shae and so it is!!!

It is truly AMAZING what the Creator has brought together for the purpose of sharing and showing Love and Adoration.

I have been a witness to so many wonderful and awesome things that can only be described as Miraculous Wonders of The Almighty and I have shed many tears of joy over them; I rejoice with the recipients of The Creator's Promises. As I recently shared in the commitment ceremony of a beloved spiritual friend of mine, I revisited the eternal mantra: what God has joined together, let no man put asunder. I began to realize that it echoes in my soul for a reason. I realized that this adage, this scriptural passage, this personal testament can be APPLIED to every area of my life!!!

Since our conception, we have been blessed with talents, gifts, and astounding capabilities to accomplish any and everything we need and want to do!!! The Creator has brought us together with the very ESSENCE of who we are. Just like a marriage, we ought to protect it and not allow for anything or anyone to come into its nucleus and destroy its foundation!!!

Let NO ONE put asunder any and all dreams and ideas that exist for the betterment and enrichment of one's soul and time on this side of creation!!!

Let NO ONE put asunder the gentleness and sweet character of the Holy Spirit and what IT has revealed to one's soul as its purpose and plans for matriculation and upliftment!!!

Let NO ONE put asunder the goals and aspirations that dwell deep within the subconscious mind. They are waiting to be released into the universe and made manifest into a tangible reality!!!

Let NO ONE put asunder the desire and the yearning to be, to have, and to express ONE'S TRUE SELF in the fullness and totality in which it ought to be!!!

Let NO ONE put asunder the financial independence and social equity that one is ENTITLED to simply because they are born as a human being and not because of conditions others may place on it!!!

Let NO ONE put asunder the genuine connection between The Creator and The Creation, no matter if others may not understand or accept its validity!!!

The time has come for all of creation to utilize the power that is INNATELY ours: the Power to CALL

FORTH WHAT NEEDS TO BE and LET NO ONE PUT ASUNDER what has already been ordained by the CREATOR!!!

Be blessed and BE A BLESSING to others!!!

The Most Important DAY of the Christian Experience

Ahhhh, Easter Sunday! This is a time when many folks are coloring eggs, getting chocolate bunnies ready to eat, and of course, buying the new suit, dress, or bonnet to wear to church. This is a time where many church folks get together and talk about those who have not been to church since LAST Easter while celebrating the Resurrection of the Christ and we sing in jubilation that HE is RISEN!!!

This is the MOST IMPORTANT DAY of the Christian Experience, as well as the most important day for those who do not necessarily consider themselves Christians but still follow the teachings of Christ. It is because of THIS DAY that all that God promised to his creation would come into fruition. It is because we understand that Jesus, at any time, could have NOT GONE THROUGH with this calling and returned to his rightful place alongside the Creator that this celebration should be like no other. If Jesus had opted out of this, then GRACE and MERCY, as we know it, would not be upon us; our existence would be something completely different. Many of us have read what times were like for those back in the days of the OLD TESTAMENT...remember when Jesus walked, there was no NEW testament because JESUS IS the New Testament. Jesus went through the fire so that WE could come out as GOLD!!! Jesus

SACRIFICED himself for US in order for US to get the benefits that GOD promised.

What a metaphor for life!!! Knowing that the task was daunting, miserable, hard, painful, dehumanizing, humiliating, ridiculous, and for some, in VAIN, Jesus STILL continued to the end because it's the OUTCOME that counts and matters MOST!!! SALVATION!!!

If only WE could learn how to do what HE did in our EVERYDAY lives without giving up or giving in! The beauty is, because of RESURECTION SUNDAY, we are given another chance, and in some cases, MANY chances to get it right so that we can receive the benefits of our labor!!!

Resurrection Sunday, as I like to refer to it, is about knowing that ALL things can be overcome and conquered!!! It is because of THIS DAY; Jesus rose and said that HE has CONQUERED HELL and HELL IS NO MORE!!! It is because of THIS DAY, we know that NO ONE CAN PUT ME THERE, but ME!!! As Elder Claude Bowen put it, "Hell is not a destination, but a state of mind!"

Resurrection Sunday also allows for us to connect with the Christ Spirit and to embrace ALL of the teachings that He has brought forth. It gives resurgence to all of those things that we have put asunder for someone else and not ourselves: those dreams that were lost, those commitments that were broken, those promises that were broken. WE as believers HAVE THE POWER to RISE UP above situations and circumstances that are out to KILL our spirits...the situations and circumstances that ROB us of JOY, LOVE, PEACE, HAPPINESS, GOODNESS, MERCY, POWER, and our very ESSENCE.

Just as God LIVES inside our hearts and our spirits, WE are also in RESURRECTION mode. Allow the Christ Spirit that is alive in you to resurrect those ideas, concepts, and gifts that were given to you for the GLORIFYING of the CREATOR!!! Allow for the Christ Spirit to RESURRECT in you a NEW ATTITUDE in order for you to RECEIVE ALL that God has to offer! Allow for the Christ Spirit to RESURRECT in you the connection to God that you thought was gone.

This is more than just eggs, chocolate bunnies, and the jubilation of the RISEN CHRIST...this is UNDERSTANDING that the RISEN CHRIST still needs to RISE in you as well!!! Embrace you inheritance and LIVE IN IT!!!

You know, LIFE is so simple that it's complex...L.I.F.E.=Love Is For Everyone!!!

Once we understand that point on this RESURECTION SUNDAY, we will be able to remove all those things that keep us bound and we will TRULY understand when Jesus said, "I have CONQUERED hell and hell is no more."

AWAKENING:

MY SPIRIT

How Do I Define POWER in My Life?

I am tremendously elated when I am able to expound on a principle or concept and share my ideas with others who are seeking uplifting and encouragement. Although we are all individuals with our unique journey ahead of us, I find it fascinating, as well as an honor and a privilege, when I can render a jewel or two of MY wisdom. What's even more beautiful is that MY wisdom doesn't have to be YOUR wisdom; however, if there is anything you find here that can benefit your journey, I implore you to apply it to your life and bless others with it.

Once, when I was sharing my wisdom with others, I was asked this question: "How do you define POWER in your life?"

When we talk about POWER, it is a concept that can be taken lightly. Many of us have allowed our environment to define and describe POWER to us; this is why we are seeking some foreign entity that may not exist in the manner we expect it. POWER is a very intoxicating and alluring concept and principle. It has a very tainted dark side if not used for enlightenment and affirmation. The examples we see on television, in the news, throughout our leadership, and within our communities have magnified POWER's darkness with very little promise for its TRUE countenance to radiate.

I often say that some concepts are so simple that they are Complexed, and POWER is one of those concepts. Since it is so simple, we have accepted all of the complexity because we are afraid of actually looking at ITS power!!!!

As for my journey along this side of creation known as life, I define POWER as being completely in tune with mind, body, and spirit! This answer may be a bit cheeky, but again, it's so simple it's complexed...I will explain.

In order for my power to be released, I MUST be living in the ABSOLUTE TRUTH of who I am! That includes accepting ALL of me, flaws and perceived flaws included because they are a part of my essence; to deny any part of me denies ALL of me!!! My mind must be clear and free from quandaries in order to recognize my surroundings. My mind must be clear to make EFFECTIVE, EFFERVESCENT DECISIONS for my life that will propel me FORWARD to achieve the goals that I have set!

In order for my power to be released, I MUST be willing to learn all I can about ME and the world I live in. KNOWLEDGE is power and what you do with it is POWERFUL!!! If I refuse to allow myself to grow and learn, then I deny myself access to my power base!!! If I refuse to surrender to my creativity, then I deny myself access to developing a solid relationship with the CREATOR and with MYSELF, therefore asking misery and contriteness to abide with me.

In order for my power to be released, I MUST be in constant connection with my spiritual self in order to sustain myself and in order to calm the world around me when the winds of peril and distress are raging. I MUST be thankful for what I have learned, accomplished, and established. I MUST listen for answers to guide me to the next level of existence!!! If I refuse to connect with my inner spirit, then I sever and destroy the foundation of my existence from all that I have been blessed by the CREATOR to build; therefore I am asking for all to fall and crumble into the abyss!!

Once I have connected all of these pieces, POWER in and for my life is established and no longer will I relinquish MY power and allow NEGATIVE ENERGY, NEGATIVE PEOPLE, and NEGATIVE CIRCUMSTANCES TO DEFINE who I am!!! NO LONGER will NEGATIVE PEOPLE, NEGATIVE CIRCUMSTANCES, or NEGATIVE ENERGY be WELCOMED in my world. Those who practice those NEGATIVE principles will WILLINGLY relieve themselves from my presence with ease and in LOVE!

Once I have connected all of these pieces, I can then utilize my POWER to be an ASSET to the community and to HUMANITY by being a servant to the people. I WILL let AGAPE LOVE reign supreme as the CREATOR has ordained us to do!

Once I have connected all of these pieces, I can ENJOY my life and I WILL have the POWER to change all of the things that I do not like about my life. I WILL continue to GROW in ABSOLUTE TRUTH to make this side of life better for me and for those I encounter.

That's how I define POWER in my life...how do you define it for YOUR life?

I AM NOT YOUR GOD!!!

As I ponder what my next move will be to advance myself closer to my goals and aspirations, I reflect on a conversation I had on a movie set with another actor. As we were talking, she and I were exchanging encouraging words of love and support in addition to sharing testaments of what we have experienced along our journeys. As she was explaining how she ALWAYS put folks in front of her and her needs, I was encouraging her to change her thinking. In our dealings with all people, even with our own children, we MUST be able to drink from the fountain of fruitfulness FIRST in order to be of use to our family.

She then proceeded to explain the flip side of that coin: when being a caregiver becomes being an ENABLER and when people, including our children, look to us for EVERYTHING! Then she said, "I AM NOT YOUR GOD"...you can run to me and expect me to save you! BAMMMMMMMM!!!!

It was at that moment that I felt as if a truckload of bricks hit me and that my soul had been set afire! That was such a PROFOUND statement and it connected my pieces for me. You see, I am one of those people who believe in caring for people and I've done so to a fault. The fault being that I neglected ME for their sake!

When I would pray, I was asking the ULTIMATE

DIVINE to show me how to not get in his/her/its way. I thought I was helping GOD, when in actuality I WAS BEING GOD!!! A-ha...that's the piece that was missing from my evaluation and introspection!

Whenever I allowed for people to come to me for EVERYTHING: from a pat on the back to spiritual development, without steering them into a place of self-realization and responsibility, I BECAME THEIR GOD!!! Each time I allowed myself to be put into situations where I became the go-to person for ALL the answers, seen and unseen, and allowed myself to BE THE CRUTCH between reality and fantasy for people, I WAS BEING THEIR GOD!!! Whenever I took it upon myself to SOLVE their problems CONTINOUSLY and allowed them to put their headaches, woes, and sorrows on MY desk without challenging them to solve them and think for themselves, I WAS BEING THEIR GOD!!! In doing so, I halted the process for each person to find GOD for themselves!!! In doing so, these people pulled from MY faith and depleted MY surplus and inherently looked to ME and not the Ultimate Divine Creator!!!

No, I am NOT your GOD!!!

See, for far too long, I have been allowing people to set their expectations on ME and I LIVED UP TO THEM in an effort to 'nurture them and show them unconditional love'. The truth of the matter is that I had/have not healed from the internal wounds of abandonment, shame, guilt, and feelings of being unloved. I THOUGHT that I was being able to shield people from that kind of pain, when in actuality; I was doing more HARM than good!!! By 'shielding' people from such things, I then ended up creating a much bigger problem...CO-DEPENDENCY; not only for them, but for me as well. I used those people to fortify my existence. I used them to define and to be my purpose in life. I used them to hide behind them whenever I was lonely, sad, afraid, and living in the low self. This vicious cycle seemed to be never-ending. The more I resented what the relationship had become, the stronger the hold was; the pain of feeling 'if I stop now, they would not love me anymore' intensified!!! Each time I would get upset because someone did not follow the instructions I had given them to handle a situation, the cycle would revolve even faster, keeping me locked into believing that this was a PERMANENT REALITY!!

No, I am NOT your GOD!!!

What I am most thankful for from The Ultimate Divine Creator is that the Sweet Spirit allowed me to SEE ME, the REAL ME, and come to myself. That PRECIOUS SPIRIT supplied the Strength I needed to pick myself up and LIVE!!! I was able to SEE ME, a Co-Creator, and break free from a delusional reality and seek TRUTH in order to RECREATE the world in which I lived. I was able to SEE ME and know that I DEFINE my purpose as I learn and ascertain my uniquely-designed journey. I am able to SEE ME as a beautiful creature entitled to ALL that is offered and promised by THE GREAT and ULTIMATE DIVINE CREATOR simply because it's my birthright!! Thank you, Mother/Father God!

No, I am NOT your GOD!!!

Understanding that we are all here to be of service to one another, we MUST be in balance with what our innate purpose is and realize our need to belong to the collective. Balance is the key to living on this side of creation as it prepares you for returning to The Spirit when you are called home.

It is okay to say to people, NO, I AM NOT YOUR GOD!!! I am GOD'S CREATION, just like YOU!!! Tap into that source for yourself and see how delightful it is to enjoy what GOD has for YOU!

In What LOVE do you OPERATE?

This question may seem as if I am talking out of the side of my neck, but I ask this question to anyone who considers what I am offering because one may believe and feel as if this is an easy question to be answered. However, I beg to differ.

You see, many may know about the term 'UNCONDTIONAL LOVE' and believe that this is the only kind of love that exists in the universe, but we ALL know that it isn't - yet we still conduct ourselves as if it is.

Let me take a moment to offer this first: there are four types of LOVE that govern us. Two of which we know…the other two we've experienced and are acting in, but we are unaware of what they are.

AGAPE: The most famous love of them all and the kind of love in which most people believe they function under. Additionally, this kind of love is the ROOT of the other kinds. This is LOVE that is UNCONDITIONAL and comes directly from The Creator. To operate in this love means that regardless of what a person says or does, the love one shows him/her is on the same level as one would show one's self or those who are a member of one's inner circle. Usually, those who profess some connection to a religious dogma or philosophy see themselves as operating in this style of love.

EROS: This kind of love is the one most people know and recognize as being different from AGAPE because to operate in this kind of love, one is ready to deal with romance, passion, lust, and carnality. Many already accept this kind of love as commonplace because it's easy for them to separate these feelings. Because of the connections made under this kind of love, AGAPE is interwoven into the fabric of a relationship because of the bond created in EROS.

PHILIA: This kind of love many don't know by name, but they know it by action. This kind of love operates as a conductor of trust and sincerity one that establishes with family and friends. Those who operate under this kind of love demonstrate loyalty and trustworthiness to those they feel have earned a place in their heart or inner circle. This kind of love is a tester for all types of relationships and becomes a blueprint for how we interact with others on a daily basis.

XENIA: This kind of love is the love that no one really knows, or quite possibly cares to know about.

This kind of love is your basic, common courtesy style love that one shows to others simply for being another human being on the planet. This is the hospitality-style love that many of us WANT OTHERS to operate in, BUT we become SELECTIVE in how WE operate in and USE it!!!

Uh-OHHHHH!!! WAIT...did I just use the word SELECTIVE??? YES I DID!!! Here's the thing: MOST OF US, I believe, OPERATE in XENIA style love because IT IS THE MOST CONDITIONAL STYLE LOVE!!!

Though we SAY we love people with the Love of Jesus and such, a.k.a. AGAPE-style love, the fact is: WE DON'T!! Society has simultaneously been very hypocritical and peculiar; IT has juxtaposed the meanings and intent of these styles of LOVE.

We have become so accustomed to being given something IN EXCHANGE for our LOVE that we don't even recognize when we are doing just that. We have become so conditioned to believe that we should hug or kiss to someone WHEN they have given us gifts, valuables, and objects of desire 'til that's the ONLY TIME when we even use the words I LOVE YOU or to even show acts of kindness and compassion. Oftentimes we are too busy destroying and desecrating the relationships we've built because we are doing all things OPPOSITE of LOVE.

Let's examine a simple action: WALKING DOWN A CROWDED or NOT SO CROWDED street. If we were operating in an AGAPE-style LOVE, to say HELLO to the passersby would not be an issue. BUT instead, because we don't know the person, because we don't like their appearance, or because we perceive them to be anything other than a CHILD OF GOD, we opt NOT to speak AND we get **offended** if THEY SPEAK TO US!!! Now I'm not talking about the obvious intent to ignore badgering panhandlers who have made it a business opportunity to cajole one out of money, goods, or time. But even in those situations, we don't even acknowledge that they are A PART OF THE CREATION that The CREATOR has placed on this earth – instead, we have the audacity to treat them with disrespect, discontentment, and disgust.

Many of us only say 'I LOVE YOU' when someone DOES or GIVES us anything we think is of value or is greatly appreciated. We even say things like 'I LOVE YOU FOR buying me this car' or whatever the item is, not realizing that we have set up conditions to how we exhibit and express our love for one another.

With family, we SAY we love them unconditionally until they destroy something of importance or until they do something that will cause us to get upset with a family member. Then we harbor grudges and all kinds of trepidation towards them instead of being angry about the incident at hand and not being angry the person involved!!!

You see, XENIA-style love gives us a REASON to point fingers and to place blame because it gives us an out. As long as we have an excuse: 'See...what had happened was...and that's why I don't love you no more', then we feel justified in our actions and we don't feel as if we should be responsible for them. Here is a secret for you: any time you have to ask yourself 'What Would Jesus Do?' you are operating in this style of love!!!

Just imagine, for a minute, if we operated TOTALLY in **AGAPE LOVE**. It's in AGAPE LOVE that we learn how to rationalize situations and see the right from the wrong OBJECTIVELY. We do what's necessary to correct mistakes without analyzing people's motivations or without harboring ill will and negative thoughts. In AGAPE LOVE, we are able to FORGIVE those who have created havoc and mayhem in our lives. Though we may not keep those people close to us, we can still send them on their way. IN AGAPE

LOVE, there is hope that they will BETTER THEMSELVES and become what the INFINITE CREATOR has decreed them to be!!! In AGAPE LOVE, we would not have all of the '-ISMS' and PHOBIAS of our world. If AGAPE LOVE was in TOTAL OPERATION, we wouldn't have Democrats vs. Republicans; str8 vs. gay, skinny vs. fat, black vs. white, tall vs. short, and JIM CROW would NOT EXIST.

I encourage you to LOOK at YOUR LIFE and YOUR WORLD and really THINK about the style of LOVE in which you TRULY AND HONESTLY operate. I don't want you to examine what YOU THINK you are doing, but I want you to examine yourself IN TRUTH and then embrace and accept that truth. Afterwards, if there is something that can be changed AND YOU WANT TO CHANGE IT - DO IT!!! I'm sure your cholesterol levels will decrease, your stress levels will drop, your angina and heartburn will change significantly, and your mind and body will feel a more serene state of PEACE!!! TRY IT - I DARE you...I DOUBLE-DOG DARE YOU to try it...NO...NOT TRY - DO!

Surrender is OH SO SWEET!!!

As I ponder over some things that have been my stumbling blocks or my acts of 'living in the low self', I am reminded of a song by Diana Ross: "Surrender". Now that songs talks about the act of recognizing the yearning for partnering with someone by surrendering your love to that someone who you THINK means the world to you. However, I am at a place where I can re-evaluate the message behind that song and take it across the board and apply it to my ENTIRE life.

SURRENDER!

For some, that word brings about hesitation and resistance. Many, if not all, have been taught that to surrender is a sign of total weakness and complete vulnerability. To surrender, many believe, is to admit defeat and it epitomizes dehumanization and desperation. This belief system only promotes carnality and does not allow for the true uplifting power of SURRENDERING to enter in and transform one's life and direct one's journey.

Often times, when challenges engage us, it is only human for us to REACT in the carnal, most times the LOW SELF, which only adds to the challenge, preventing us from becoming victorious and empowered. The concept of "leaning on the higher power" becomes another church epithet and challenges are fueled by the negative energy WE gave it. Instead of allowing the HIGHER POWER to prevail and to SURRENDER to it, we RESIST it at all costs believing that it's OUR power that will sustain us and bring forth the harvest of crop, when in actuality, it only hinders us from attaining THE BEST YIELD!!!

SURRENDER!!!

The power of SURRENDER transcends all that the conscious mind can conceive. For too long, the focus has been on the negative energy of SURRENDER, but it is only when we examine all the ramifications SURRENDER offers can we ascertain its gifts. To SURRENDER is to succumb to the HIGHER POWER and allow for it to mold, shape and redirect one's path so that one can experience their FULLEST potential!! To SURRENDER is to RELEASE EVERYTHING and begin anew!!! To SURRENDER is to TRUST that the HIGHER POWER will guide one's hand throughout the creative process while developing the masterpiece known as YOUR LIFE!! To SURRENDER is to ACTIVATE and EXERCISE your FAITH!!!

Yeah, I know, this sounds easier than it is to put into action, but that feeling exist because we have become so accustomed to RESISTANCE, in addition to allowing False Evidences Appearing Real (FEAR) to be our governing force which interferes with progress. We have allowed FEAR to dictate to us what the process MAY BE instead of actually experiencing the process. We are afraid to be seen in our most vulnerable state, BUT it's only then can we begin the PROCESS TO GROW and SURRENDER everything over to our HIGHER POWER!!!

We have all heard the adage, "Let Go and Let God", and even used it, taught it to others, and even spoke it aloud as if it is the most sound advice to give to someone going through a crisis, but do we actually know what that means?

To LET GO is more than just pretty words, it is the ARTFORM of releasing all that has you bound and imprisoned. All those things which seem to be overwhelming, exacerbating, excruciating, flabbergasting, and have SIGNIFICANT POWER over your life are to be confronted and destroyed on ITS level and that is IN THE SPIRIT! It is the time to exercise strength and courage and stand NAKED before our problems and issues and accept the outcome COME WHAT MAY believing and knowing that all is for the GREATEST GOOD for one's life!!!

To LET GOD is more than just praying for something to go away! It means to open oneself up to allowing the principles of The Divine Creator to manifest themselves in your life. It's a time to allow The Creator to honor the promises he/she/it has made to THE CREATION. It is a time for Creation to sit back and watch The Creator work miracles in your life to fortify the relationship that has been established between The Creator and The Creation. It is the time where hope and possibility gets the opportunity to be heard and answered! It is the time where we are NAKED before The Creator, regaining and RECLAIMING our innocence and purity and allowing the communion of SURRENDER and The Creator's Will to align with our lives.

SURRENDER!!!

Once we combat the negative notions of SURRENDER and bask in and empower ourselves with its sweetness, the possibilities are endless as to what we can accomplish o n this side of creation, all that we can rid ourselves from that which brings about harm and destruction, how much closer and stronger our connection to the Creator we will be, and how much individual, independent freedom we will obtain, all because we learn how to SURRENDER completely, wholly and honestly!!

Be Blessed and Know that All things work TOGETHER for the GOOD!!!

The PROCESS is Sandpaper for the SOUL!

It is the end of another year, and for so long, I've been having this message bottled up inside me, however, I never knew when I was going to be able to share it with anyone. Sure, I've hinted at it a few times and I've even presented this concept to a few people close to me who understand how I operate and how my mind works...BUT the time to share it in its fullness did not reveal itself until today!

When one considers and contemplates THE PROCESS, one is often perplexed because it seems to be such a vast concept. When 'the prophetess' Juanita Bynum brought this concept to life in her No More Sheets campaign, she illustrated how the process worked in HER LIFE. But for me however, I wondered about all of the nuances of THE PROCESS: how to define it, how to relate to it, and how it affects every element of my life, across the board, without reason or rhyme. THE PROCESS is sometimes brutal, painstakingly unbearable, and oftentimes downright HATEFUL!!! Yes, I said it...it is down right HATEFUL...or at least that's how one may feel and wish to interpret those feelings.

You see, one enjoys the BENEFITS of what THE PROCESS yields, but no one wants to go THROUGH THE PROCESS because literally, it evokes the epitome of GOING TO and THROUGH HELL!!! Furthermore, what we do not want to acknowledge or accept is that THE PROCESS is a necessary tool REQUIRED to bring about our BEST AUTHENTIC SELF!

Just as a carpenter (catch that now...remember, Jesus was a carpenter) needs his tools when building a home, painting a wall, or whatever the task may be, we need our tools whenever we need to BUILD our HOMES or *TEMPLES*, if you will. We need our tools whenever we need HOME IMPROVEMENT WORK done or when a simple RENOVATION is needed for the overall appearance and maintenance of *the temple*. One of the tools needed to bring about the beauty of a smooth, polished look and feel of a project is sandpaper. Depending on how severe the project is, the grade of sandpaper becomes coarser; it needs to strip away nicks and imperfections in order to reveal the true essence of the project at hand and in order for everyone to admire its beauty.

THE PROCESS is SANDPAPER for the SOUL!

As individuals who have been scorned, bruised, tainted, dismayed, manhandled, bamboozled, hoodwinked, cajoled, and plain ole damaged, we come into any situation with preconceived notions, judgments, ridicule, and banter; this is a means to keep us from being PROCESSED. As individuals, we never view ourselves with faults and idiosyncrasies - yet we are quick to exercise our self-appointed rights to deputize ourselves as 'Fault and Sinner Police Officers' and we will give any and everyone a citation if THEY are not willing to be PROCESSED.

The PROCESS is SANDPAPER for the SOUL!

Upon accepting this challenge to become your authentic self, one must understand that there is no time limit to THE PROCESS, and most times, it's a LIFELONG PROCESS. We are growing each and every single day that we are on this side of creation. We are benefiting from the gifts of life, breath, food, shelter, water, and the carnal pleasures we've become accustomed to, yet we act as if we wouldn't know how to survive without them.

THE PROCESS is all of the waiting, stewing, cooing, booing, anxiety, nervousness, fearfulness, relentless skepticism, the questioning, the uncertainty, the endless nights of praying, the hours on the phone looking for advice from your BEST FRIEND, the anger, the frustration, the biting your tongue when you want to cuss someone out, the analyzing, the OVER analyzing, and all of the bullshit we go through, MUST go through and PUT OURSELVES THROUGH in order to seek answers and RESOLVE of a situation!

THE PROCESS is activated in a controlled environment that dictates exactly what areas need to be re-examined, reproached, rebuked, remolded, and reconciled with the collective of SELF.

THE PROCESS tears away all of the layers of grit, grime, grease, gruel, and graven behaviors that have been building up like plaque on the wall of one's inner soul.

THE PROCESS is ALWAYS COARSE so that it can completely remove all of the soot and decay from the bowels of the soul. This is necessary in order to repel the stench of heartbreak, disillusionment, abandonment, abuse, misguiding, misunderstanding, miseducation, and disenfranchising left behind that can blindly intoxicate one into an altered state of authenticity.

THE PROCESS is designed to POLISH the soul as it brings forth the TRUE ESSENCE of THE SPIRITUAL SELF. It provides comfort and solutions about how to

COEXIST with the NATURAL SELF in perfect harmony.

THE PROCESS always goes ALONG THE GRAIN. It permeates through the RESISTANCE that one has built from the gunk of pomp and circumstance that has continuously been going AGAINST THE GRAIN. This results in one developing strong defensive tactics that prevent the AUTHENTIC SELF from blossoming.

THE PROCESS is SANDPAPER for the Soul. It breaks down each layer of unjust, anti-spiritual, and antagonistic thought, feeling, action, and reaction. It purges one's heart, mind, body, and spirit.

Now once THE PROCESS begins, there is no TURNING BACK! THE PROCESS directs itself along the path of HEALING and CLEANSING and it works just like a laxative by loosening the toxins thoroughly trapped and intertwined into the fabric and cellular structure of one's existence. THE PROCESS is no respecter of persons and doesn't show favoritism because of one's social-economic background or status; it is on its mission to transcend, transmogrify, transition, and transport THE LIVING SPIRIT of the host it's working on to its HIGHEST LEVEL of EXISTENCE and INTERPRETATION!

It is only THEN that the vessel, the host, the person, the creation will be seen as the PRECIOUS JEWEL it is versus the lump of coal that has cocooned it for so long. It is THEN that THE PROCESS shows one their TRUE VALUE as a part of creation…it is THEN that one APPRECIATES, ACKNOWLEDGES, and ACCEPTS that they ARE PRICELESS!!! A'she and so it IS…and SO IT SHALL BE…

AWAKENING:

MY HUMANITY

Mr. HONESTY, a.k.a. HONEST, is a MAN OF ACTION!!!

It has been said that when two are joined together they become one. It has been my belief that for the values, morals, and principles that have molded, sculpted, and shaped our society and existence, the virtuous union, that the magnificent marriage of Mr. Honesty, a.k.a. Honest and Truth, yields the true essence of The Creator's spirit. It proves, yet again, that The Creator's purpose is ongoing and forthcoming.

Like all marriages where the husband is the head of the household, Mr. Honesty does not disappoint because Mr. Honesty, a.k.a. Honest, is a MAN of ACTION!

Mr. Honesty, a.k.a. Honest, is bold and daring. He stands up to any challenge and draws strength from staying focused on the greater goals that lie ahead.

Mr. Honesty, a.k.a. Honest, stands fast and does not allow for anything to cloud his judgment or deter him from attaining all that he sets out to do!

Mr. Honesty, a.k.a. Honest, nurtures his soul with positive influences that represent whom and what he is to remain true to: himself and his family!

Mr. Honesty, a.k.a. Honest, is a MAN of ACTION!

Mr. Honesty, a.k.a. Honest, has deeply rooted his foundation in the spirit of the Creator, believing, knowing, and trusting that ALL THINGS WORK TOGETHER FOR THE GOOD of those who Love and Respect the Power of Love and The Creator!

Mr. Honesty, a.k.a. Honest, is a family man who understands and believes in the power and the dynamic of the family unit. He stands behind and embraces, in totality, his wife TRUTH; he supports her every effort and all of her intentions. They are a UNIFIED FRONT that no man, woman, child, thought, or deed can or will put asunder!

Mr. Honesty, a.k.a. Honest, is a risk taker. He is not afraid to defend himself in honor of his value system, principles, and beliefs that define the core of his essence; HE COMMANDS attention and respect wherever he goes.

Like most MEN, Mr. Honesty, a.k.a. Honest, is a man of few words - BUT when he speaks, he speaks with distinction, conviction, and purpose. He is no Respecter of persons, titles, or accolades. Mr. Honesty, a.k.a. Honest, lays down the law and makes no excuses for doing so because if it has to be done, it NEEDED to be done!!!

Most definitely, Mr. Honesty, a.k.a. Honest, is a MAN of ACTION and should be admired, respected, and emulated. What a wonderful role model for us all: honesty.

RECLAIMING OUR CHILDREN!!!

I start this by saying: The ENEMY is NOT POWERFUL ENOUGH TO WIN THE WAR!!! WE have to STOP giving our POWER over to the enemy it as if it does!!! Negative ENERGY is present so that WE CAN IDENTIFY IT, ACCEPT what is represents, and then use it to JUMPSTART US so that we can GET ON TRACK with exuding POSITIVE energy. Then we can TRULY LIVE the life that THE INFINITE has called us to LIVE!!

The enemy has sent forth this new thing of attacking our children through those who have been the vessels that brought them into existence on this side of creation. We have been hearing too many stories of how children are being heinously attacked, mistreated, abused, and destroyed at the hands of their parents and those who they've trusted to protect and care for them. But here is something I want you to consider: the perpetrators have not only stolen the innocence of these children, but they are attempting to destroy their SPIRIT, which could prove to be a deadly blow to a spiritual body.

The time that it will take to heal from such hurt could bring about serious devastation to this planet. I'm sure you are as appalled as I am to hear when someone desecrates the spirit of a child. To KNOW that there is NOTHING that I could do about it could harden my heart and bring forth JUDGMENT and RAGE. To know that I am not alone suggests that the world is on the brink of IMPLOSION. With so much rage and anger and HATE, LOVE has a strong battle to show up and REIGN SUPREME as the ULTIMATE FORCE OF ENERGY. It is very easy for us to become JADED to LOVE because of how others have committed crimes against our greatest resources: CHILDREN.

It's very EASY for us to BLAME THE INFINITE CREATOR because we don't understand why this desecration exists or why THE INFINITE CREATOR allows for such atrocities to occur. It's very EASY for us to CURSE, MAME, and PROFANE all those who are the perpetrators of such nonsense; however, if we are TRULY following THE TEACHINGS OF CHRIST, we are supposed to LOVE these people unconditionally as well!!!

Are we becoming a world full of VENOM and MALICE? What are we teaching our CHILDREN these days? These acts of dehumanization are a travesty against ALL that is JUST and WONDERFUL IN THIS WORLD, and we have OURSELVES to thank for it!!!

For my staunch CHRISTIANS out there, scriptures tell us in Matthew 18:3-4: "I tell you the truth, unless you change and become like little children, you will never enter the kingdom of heaven. Therefore, whoever humbles himself like this child is the greatest in the kingdom of heaven".

With all of the tragedies happening to our children, it

seems that the very spirit needs to ascertain the Kingdom of Heaven. According to Christian teaching, it has been taken from us and a WAR has been declared. The problem is: WE ARE NOT doing our part to PRESERVE our CHILDREN or the inner child within US!!! Many of us have unresolved issues from childhood that have spilled over into our adult lives. This has ultimately affected how we see and deal with the world!

The time has come for us to RECLAIM OUR CHILDREN!

We MUST RECLAIM OUR CHILDREN and keep them on the forefront of the societal rings of SUCCESS AND VALOR!

We MUST RECLAIM OUR CHILDREN and re-enforce those qualities that will build character and encourage growth.

We MUST RECLAIM OUR CHILDREN and assist them in developing their creativity and in broadening their imagination so that they can continue to be UNIQUE individuals.

We MUST RECLAIM OUR CHILDREN and stimulate their growth spiritually so that they KNOW who they are and how DIVINELY CONNECTED they are to THE INFINITE CREATOR!

This hogwash of stifling of our children, hindering our children, holding our children back, and miseducating our children has run its course and the

TIME HAS COME FOR REAL PEOPLE, REAL PARENTS, and REAL NURTURERS to step up and RECLAIM OUR CHILDREN! We've got the power to do ANY AND EVERYTHING!!!

That Girl, KARMA, is a MUTHA FOR YA!!!

I have often heard it said that Motherhood is the GREATEST job on the planet. To take a new creation and nurture it along its journey...to watch, with wanting eyes, the development of such a creation! To watch a child blossom and flourish into something beyond expectation is a great triumph for any parent who participates in their child's life.

Well, let me introduce you to a Mutha beyond all mothers...a mother who allows her children to be exactly what they are destined to become!!!

That girl KARMA...yeah, she's a MUTHA for ya!!!

KARMA is a bonafide country girl. She's a Sophisticated Lady who was born and raised to tend the farmland. She believes in gentle love and never raises her voice or her hand to get her point across.

KARMA works hard to make sure that all that you have planted comes to FULL HARVEST in its own time.

KARMA works the land in which you have planted your seeds and never questions if the seed is of positive or negative fruit!!

KARMA makes sure that the land, soil, and crop is cared for so that you are not disappointed with your return.

KARMA, like any other MUTHA, makes sure that her children's needs are not neglected or compromised.

Yeah, BABY...that Girl KARMA is a Mutha for ya!!!

KARMA is any man's delight because she is obedient. She will make sure that you get EXACTLY what you asked for.

KARMA is any child's' friend because she is a Protector and watches over her flock with a steady eye and open ears, slowly teaching them about planting seeds and harvesting the crop in which they yield.

KARMA is an ambassador for spiritual growth as she is constantly connected to the DIVINE.

KARMA is molded after the CREATOR'S Spirit because she is not respecter of persons. She is an Equal Opportunity Enforcer and PROUDLY displays her badge of armor.

I told you...that Girl KARMA is a Mutha for ya!!!!

KARMA will gracefully and willingly produce whatever the harvest brings forth.

KARMA will allow for her children to rant and rave without judgement or recall because they may not be happy with the crop that has been yielded.

KARMA exercises discipline and tough love. She will allow for her children to walk away in disbelief and dismay, never blaming herself for the outcome of the harvest, for she KNOWS she brought forth what YOU planted.

KARMA doesn't condemn or damn anyone for the seeds they plant - she just nurtures them and brings the yield to fruition because it's obvious that it was YOUR CHOICE to plant those seeds.

And the effervescent beauty of KARMA is that she will always grant you the opportunity to DO IT ALL over again, and like any mutha, she will coast you to planting better seeds for a better harvest in the future.

Yes, Lord...that Girl KARMA is a Mutha for ya!!!

Time IS On Our Side!!!

In today's world, where everything seems to be governed by the 24 hours in the day, and because never-ending tasks make it seem as if we never have enough time to do it all, I have discovered the secrets to understanding how to have ENOUGH TIME to do any and everything that must be done in my life. Now, you may say to yourself, "What the hell is he talking about? No one gets everything done," and in some instances, you may be right. BUT in order for us not to be consumed with the time getting away from us, we MUST accept and recognize a few principles regarding time in order to appreciate and to receive the benefits that Time has to offer.

Principle 1: TIME can and will be your friend.

One of the reasons that we never have enough Time is because we are too busy making Time an ENEMY or an adversary and not an Ally or a FRIEND. Once we accept TIME as our friend and begin to do so from the precise moment we make this introduction, TIME becomes our vantage point. We will no longer 'race against TIME' because there is nothing in which we must compete.

TIME becomes our friend once we realize and begin to live in the NOW versus being caught up in the YESTERDAY of our journey. It is our responsibility to appreciate the MOMENTS in which we live so that we don't miss out on the blessings that each moment brings. TIME shares those blessings with us as a friend would by allowing us the opportunity to experience it in its fullness - COME WHAT MAY!!!

Principal 2: TIME's Essence is a Metaphor for LIVING!

If we stop to examine TIME and how it operates, we can apply its essence to our own lives and we can become more effective and productive citizens. Let's look at how TIME operates:

TIME ALWAYS moves forward...it never looks back.

TIME moves with or without anyone's participation, consent, or analysis of any situation or factor.

TIME doesn't stop and become hindered by other's hesitation, resistance, or fear.

TIME never gets in anyone's business because TIME is constantly focused on its goal.

TIME knows that once a moment is gone, it's gone forever and is only a memory. Therefore, TIME is looking forward to creating NEW memories and NEW moments while welcoming NEW experiences.

Principle 3: TIME is no respecter of persons!!!

It doesn't matter if you are rich/poor, black/white, gay/straight, young/old, male/female and any other combination, or opposite entity and the liking, TIME reacts to all of us the SAME!!! TIME is one of the concepts that unite us all because it speaks to all of us in the same language: FREEDOM and EQUALITY!!!

YES, Time IS on our side. Once we believe that statement, we can move forward WITH and IN TIME to accomplish ALL of the things that will generate and promote our BEST SELVES.

Here's the thing that seems to escape us: TIME is a spiritual entity with a human concept. TIME exists because our human minds have developed a tangible measurement in an effort to understand it. Once we begin to release ourselves from the bondage of time management and linear existence can we then free ourselves from the agony of worry, fear, and restlessness of being inadequate, inferior, and abnormal.

TIME IS WHAT WE MAKE OF IT!!! If you truly embrace it, then YES! TIME IS ON OUR SIDE.

Truth is a BAD BITCH!!!

Everyday, as I evolve into the awakenings of my life and from my experiences which allow me to be FREE, I have discovered that LIVING IN TRUTH is a concept that transcends BEYOND this world! As I realize the complete and awesome POWER of TRUTH, I am accepting TRUTH as MY new SUPERHERO!!! Yeah, that's right!!! TRUTH is a BAD BITCH...and I thank her for it!!!

See, TRUTH is the only loner who can stand alone and not give a damn whether or not your accept her or agree with her!

TRUTH does not need to be affirmed or justified because she is what she is: TRUTH!

TRUTH does not need to be co-signed, praised, or defended because she stands in her own light and EDIFICATION!

TRUTH is FAT FREE with no colors, flavors, additives, or preservatives!!!

TRUTH is ALL NATURAL and does a body, person, and humanity GOOD!!!

Yeah, TRUTH is a BAD BITCH!!!

TRUTH uplifts and encourages EVERYONE to BE, LIVE, and EXPERIENCE the BEST that life has to offer!!!

TRUTH is a fighter of justice…and she fights without putting up a sweat!!!

TRUTH crushes and destroys fiction, fables, lies, and deceit!!!

Oh Yeah, TRUTH is a BAD BITCH!!!

TRUTH does not allow for NEGATIVITY to gain momentum or become a beacon of falsehood!

TRUTH may be a loner, but she always welcomes friendships and alliances. She will accept and protect those who will accept her with open arms!

Yes, Lord…TRUTH is a BAD BITCH!!!

TRUTH nurtures the soul and will allow for anyone to ease into TRUTH's comfort zone!

TRUTH accepts, acknowledges, and understands that she is not always the EASY ROAD and she does not make excuses for it!!!

TRUTH knows she is rough around the edges and can be a hard pill to swallow, and she makes no excuses for it!!!

Yeah, TRUTH is a BAD BITCH!!!

TRUTH allows you to USE her power to accomplish your growth potential...BUT she will not stand for ANYONE ABUSING her power because, Truthfully speaking, to abuse TRUTH is not LIVING IN TRUTH...it's living in SIN (SELF INFLICTED NONSENSE)!

You see what I mean...TRUTH IS A BAD BITCH!!!

TRUTH is both OBJECTIVE and SUBJECTIVE; she allows for humanity to embrace her as a whole and she still allows for individuals to WAKE UP and understand their own journey through life.

TRUTH dispels myths, rhetoric, dogmas, traditions, rituals, and ceremonies!

That's right...TRUTH is a BAD BITCH!!!

The one thing that most folk don't get is that TRUTH doesn't care if you accept or deny her, fuss and fight with her, stand her up, or be standoffish with her. She KNOWS, when it's all said and done, that YOU WILL come to HER with open arms IN TRUTH...ready, able, and prepared to EMBRACE HER!!!

YEAH, BABY...TRUTH IS A BAD BITCH!!!

WHAT Are You THANKFUL For?

Every year, as the holiday season approaches, I experience a great deal of trepidation. My spirit does not seem to gel well with the concept of a SINGLE day or SEASON in which we, as a people, realize that others are in need and that many are at a point of hopelessness and despair.

I do UNDERSTAND WHY the holiday season is most infectious with all of the LOVE in the air: the feeling of satisfaction one receives knowing they have made a difference in the lives of others, sharing a piece of one's heart with someone that one would otherwise have never shared, and the JOY of being engulfed in the spirit of PEACE and EUPHORIA as one experiences caring for someone other than one's self. A good spiritual friend of mine told me that we should be thankful that, at least one time during the year, the masses concentrate on those who are in need of service and we should let THAT spirit prevail; it will keep evil from being the most dominate sentiment across the land during the MOST IMPORTANT time of the year. I thought that I was going to acquiesce to that point; however, I can't seem to fully accept that reasoning. I have found that this line of thinking is fuel for those who capitalize on this season. They manipulate, juxtapose, and connive their way into a 'blessing' so that they can 'BE THANKFUL' for the stunts and shenanigans working in their favor.

I am at a point in my life (and I hope others will get to this point as well or at least a derivative of it) where the pomp and circumstance of 'The Holiday Season' is becoming more of a gimmick and less about actually being of good service to humankind to build a better place for ALL of us. The 'gimmick' I'm referring to is the illusion that because one is showing kindness during this time of year that it means that they are 'Being of Good Cheer', 'Doing What Jesus Would Do', and associating themselves with any other proverbial phrase that would culminate in the idea of being viewed as a good person. For many, this is a sincere moment and a blissful time of year; they have been actively participating in servitude throughout the year and it has become a lifestyle for them. But those who CONVENIENTLY don the cape and mask of 'Rescue Ranger' are the ones who damper this time of year and bring about speculation and pause.

In addition to this, there are the never-ending clichés that sound like an autonomous response whenever dinner is served. The blessing is said and the question is raised: What are you Thankful For?

Are you really thankful for family and friends to share this holiday with? Do you laugh, love, and create special long-lasting memories with them as you embrace and encourage one another to succeed? OR is this just something to say because you really can't stand them and you hope that they will hurry this thing along so you can eat as much as you can before fixing a to go plate?

Are you really thankful for your children who have brought you joy, taught you how to be patient and loving, demonstrated that they LOVE you unconditionally, and are a mirror of the behaviors YOU exhibit in an effort to bring about change for improvement? OR are you being kind because you secretly wished that you had aborted them and/or you really didn't care for the person who assisted you in bringing them into the world despite the fact that they are a by-product of your carnality?

Are you really thankful for a roof over your head to call home? OR are you being kind because you are a freeloader taking up space in someone's home? Are you refusing to pull your own weight or do you have to be told to clean up or wash a dish EXPECTING your host to 'help a brutha/sistah out cuz you know it's hard out there'?

Are you REALLY thankful for The INFINITE CREATOR allowing you to see another day while holding you in loving arms of protection and showering you with abundance and blessings? OR are you being kind because you have determined that your 'convenient benevolence' is your 'BUY MYSELF INTO HEAVEN CARD'? Throughout the holiday season, are you keeping up appearances so the outside world would think you are such a 'strong person of God'?

Imagine what this world would be like if we stopped attempting to gain brownie points with The Infinite Creator and started to genuinely BE OF SERVICE TO ONE ANOTHER!!! The Soup Kitchens and Homeless Shelters would not have to beg for volunteers year-round and then have a barrage of volunteers during 'the holiday season' that they have to TURN AWAY because of the sudden and abundant influx!!!

Imagine what the world would be like if we adopted a family, not just at Thanksgiving and Christmas, but year-round so that they know that someone has their back. They would know that someone encourages them to move forward as a family without the threat of parents splitting up or children being forced away from their parents!!!

Imagine what the world would be like if we CONTINOUSLY showed random acts of kindness - not just the sympathetic dollar bill toss to a nameless stranger one sees right after leaving a soul-stirring church service.

Imagine what the world would be like if we completely embraced our heritage HONESTLY and INCLUSIVELY. What if we constantly showed our pride by how we treated one another? What if we accepted one another's differences while celebrating our similarities? What if we just stopped waiting until KWANZAA, PASSOVER, HANNAKAH, GAY PRIDE MONTH, and any other special day set aside to honor a specific culture where the celebration is criticized and ridiculed because the masses don't understand WHY IT EXISTS???

What I am thankful for is how I AM A PART OF THIS THING CALLED LIFE...ORDAINED BY THE INFINITE CREATOR and PLACED IN THIS TIME AND SPACE TO BE MY AUTHENTIC SELF REGARDLESS OF HOW OTHERS PERCEIVE AND RECEIVE ME!!!

I am thankful for those who are in my life to keep me GROUNDED and who are not afraid to challenge me, inspire me to grow into my fullness, and who accept my brand of humor and my reasoning process.

I am thankful for THE POWER TO DREAM AND VISUALIZE things into existence…THE POWER to CREATE the WORLD I WANT for ME and those who are STRONG ENOUGH TO ACCEPT coexisting with me!!!

I am thankful for THE OMNIVERSE…for without it, NOTHING CAN OR WILL EXIST!!! Its vastness is OVERWHELMING and INDESCRIBABLE - yet it is ALL-INCLUSIVE and is in requirement of MY CONTRIBUTIONS in order to Sustain ITSELF!!! There is no separation from it…WHAT A GIFT that is - to be UNIQUELY and INDIVIDUALLY DESIGNED to function INDEPENDENTLY and yet STILL be part of the COLLECTIVE!!!

FOR THIS I AM ETERNALLY THANKFUL AND GRATEFUL!!!

What Is the Difference?

I wrote this essay on Father's Day 2009, and I wanted to share it with you.

It's Father's Day and I am sharing this offering with you; I wanted to bring forth my version of a blueprint for Fatherhood. Now this is too funny because I am NOT a biological father and many of you may feel as if I don't have the credentials or the qualifications to render advise or counsel. HOWEVER, since I have been a OMNIVERSAL PARENT in this culture, I do have a commentary that I believe would bring forth dialogue, and PRAYERFULLY, an ACTION PLAN that would catapult a revolution in the MALE SPECIES!!!

I asked this question to an online group and NO ONE answered it substantially because we've all been bombarded with the internalized pain and hurt associated with it:

What is the Difference between a Father, a Daddy, and a Sperm Donor?

Well, I believe it is simple; but like most things, it's so simple, it's complexed!!! Oftentimes, I truly believe that the terms 'Father' and 'Daddy' have been intertwined or juxtaposed when they are two separate things!

A Father is the one who has LIMITED involvement in the life of a child. He usually doesn't mean to be the isolated parent, but due to obligations and prior commitments, He is only there for financial support and limited emotional support. A father will put discipline in place and will enforce it, but he may become lax in his responsibilities with it.

A Daddy is the one who becomes TOTALLY involved in the development of a child's existence. A daddy is the one who encourages the social skills of the child, enhances the ideals of family togetherness, and instills a sense of pride and integrity in his child or children. A daddy nurtures the creativity of the child and assists in the development of all gifts and talents that will sustain a child's livelihood. A Daddy nourishes a child's beliefs, fortifies a child's spirit, and edifies a child's-self esteem. A Daddy provides EMOTIONAL AND FINANCIAL support and UNCONDITIONAL LOVE for the child/children without hesitation or pause. A Daddy also disciplines in Truth, Love, and when necessary. A DADDY is not afraid to challenge his children to be their best and doesn't fold when times are hard and sour.

A Sperm Donor is the one with the most grief attached to his persona. A Sperm Donor has NOTHING to do with the child/children except for providing the seed for germination. It sounds very crude, but it's oh so true...like I said earlier, it's so simple it's complexed. Oftentimes, A Sperm Donor is equated with the likes of a Pimp, Baller, Rolling Stone, Deadbeat Dad, and many other euphemisms associated with non-parental involvement. In many instances, a Sperm Donor is viewed as a male whore looking to substantiate his masculinity by taking the population of the world to a whole new high!!! A Sperm Donor wants bragging rights to having 'fathered' children, but he takes NO RESPONSIBILITY in the children's welfare. What most people fail to understand is that he, too, has a purpose: a Sperm Donor is the vessel used to carry out The Creator's plan for bringing forth the child!

All of us know people who fall into one of the three categories I talked about, but the real question becomes this: when will MEN stand up and take their RIGHTFUL PLACE in a child's heart? Once we learn how to do that, MY BRUTHAS, without getting mixed up in what constitutes masculinity, can we begin to produce a healthier world and a more stable foundation for our offspring.

This goes out to all who are Fathers, Big Daddies, Uncles, Stepfathers, Mentors, and Big Bruthas who have stepped in and helped to shape the life of a child or the life of anyone that you've taken under your wing!

HAPPY FATHER'S DAY to YOU!!!

For those of you who hold anger and feel despair for the Sperm Donor who has not been a guiding force in your life, we will CELEBRATE him has well...for without HIM...there is NO YOU!!!

SO to all my Sperm Donors out there, if you don't do anything else, YOU ALREADY DONE ENOUGH!!! So, thank you for getting ME here!!!

For my single bruthas who don't have biological children but have been a surrogate father and mentor to a myriad of children and some adults you have encountered...for those of you who have built families for runaways and for those who were deemed lost or have been rejected by their families...you too are acknowledged on THIS DAY!

Celebrate the life of your FATHER today! Do more than giving power tools and sporting goods - PLEASE...HONOR HIM, CHERISH HIM, and BASK in HIM today!!!

AWAKENING:

TO ME

AN AFFIRMATION OF SELF TO SELF, FOR SELF, BY SELF

There are times when the need to talk to oneself is apparent and, in most cases, NEEDED in order to sustain one's thoughts and actions. This also preserves the good nature and intent in which your purpose dwells.

It is then that one should be compelled to STOP, LOOK, and LISTEN to what's being said from within. Then one should APPLY the lessons or instructions given to in order to facilitate and fortify one's existence and plight to continue on one's journey.

I offer this affirmation as a beginning to the process of LEARNING HOW TO LOVE YOURSELF and after which you will TEACH others how to love you.

Stand in front of a mirror and LOOK at yourself; then align your heart and your mind to these words:

I stand before you in the wholeness and totality of MY ESSENCE and I welcome it into MY LIFE without hesitation.

I know I am created in the IMAGE, the DIVINE IMAGE of the Infinite Creator and I cannot and will not give anything else POWER over what and who I am.

I know that because I am created in the IMAGE of the Infinite Creator that I, too, have been given the POWER to create and the POWER to do all things that will sustain me on this side of creation.

I will NOT give credence to anything that holds me captive or imprisons me. I will NOT give credence to any other Image that is not representative of who I am and that will interfere with my divinity with The Creator.

I acknowledge that at this moment that I AM FINE just as I am, regardless of what others may say, what society may deem as perfection, and what humankind may ridicule and criticize...I AM because the CREATOR IS...

I remind myself that I hold the POWER to change that which does not promote a healthy journey or that which does not support who and what I am!

I remind myself and EMPOWER myself to UNDERSTAND AND KNOW that through my faults and fears, my anguish and despair...NOTHING can separate me from the LOVE of the CREATOR. Simply because I exist, this PROVES that I am ENTITLED to it freely without guilt, discord, reproach, or refinement!

I accept and KNOW it is OKAY to BE ME...the REAL ME....the WHOLE ME....the AUTHENTIC ME...and I don't have to explain it to ANYONE....

I AM WHAT AND WHO I SAY I AM, WHAT AND WHO I THINK I AM, WHAT AND WHO I BELIEVE I AM, AND WHAT AND WHO I KNOW I AM! BLESS THE DIVINE CREATOR FOR IT ALL!!

The Darker Side of SEX!!!

I've decided to share my story with you because it is a part of MY healing and releasing!!! It is important that we ALL learn and understand that life's experiences are not to keep us from our potential, but they are to BUILD us to BE our potential!!! As you read this, I implore you to THINK about your own experiences and how you have or have not dealt with them and then take this time to DO SOMETHING to HEAL YOURSELF!!!

I chose NOT to hide from this as it WAS a part of me, and in some regards, still IS as I venture to help those who struggle with it!!! Many may feel as if I am putting too much of my business in the streets...well, my darling, I have nothing to hide any more and I WILL NOT let something that has NO FOUNDATION in my life DICTATE my life!!!

It is when we come out of the closets and from under the covers, blankets, and umbrellas of shame and ridicule that we, as human beings, will understand that it took this experience to Mold and Shape me into who I am today!!! YES, it was HELL...pure, unadulterated HELL...but like JESUS did, I CONQUERED HELL! Whenever I find myself in that space again, (knowing that I have and still do get MYSELF into those kinds of situations), I have to COME TO MYSELF, RECOGNIZE my powerbase, and bring MYSELF out of the situation, which was THE

HELL that I had created!!!

This is a RAW, HONEST look at addiction from MY experiences. No one under the age of consent should read this without supervision!!!

The Darker Side of Sex!!!

"Oh, yes, Big Daddy, fuck me!!! Don't stop fucking me, baby!"

"Who's ass is this, nigga! Who fucking this Ass?"

"Take what you want, Daddy! Bang this muthafuckin' ass, nigga!"

"Yeah, boi...oooh, shit, this dick is good!!!"

"This my pussy...ain't it, bitch!"

"Shoot that shit all over me, Daddy!"

"Suck dat dick real good, boy..."

"Awww, shit, I'm bout to bust...I'm bout to cum, baby!!!"

Take this cum, bitch....take all this cum..."

Yeah, this brings back some memories or could possibly get you wondering if you can make a call right now....doesn't it? See, this is the side of sex that we all adore. The fun side, the wild side…being with someone whether they are a lover, fuck buddy, or a cute piece you just picked up to add a notch on your belt. We enjoy it just for the sheer enjoyment of it all, and afterwards, we love to share those stories with our closest friends or write about the experiences in our journals. But there is a side to all of this that haunts many of us and I am one of those people.

You know it is true…SEXUAL ADDICTION is real!!! Many folks don't believe that it exists. Folks feel that it is a playful way of saying that a person wants to be a 'ho' or that a person really enjoys having sex with many different partners.

I am here to tell you that it is REAL!!! The uncontrollable urge to want to deeply penetrate someone, or to get plunged by someone, or to have that nagging feeling of needing to have a dick down your throat or some ass in your face for hours on end…yeah, this may seem like a normal feeling for someone who is probably in dire straits because they have been without for a minute or two. But when IT controls YOU and you cannot maintain your sense of self or your peace of mind is when it is problematic. Whenever you find yourself going above and beyond what you would normally do to have sex is when you have to realize something is wrong: talking yourself out of using or NOT USING CONDOMS when you normally would…HAVING SEX WITH SOMEONE YOU KNOW IS HIV-POSITIVE AND NOT

PROTECTING YOURSELF...going into dark alleys lurking around for anyone who is willing to go there with you...walking aimlessly around parks and all the hot spots looking for a piece when there is no one there and LINGERING around for fear that if you leave you might miss out on something...fear of rejection from the one you want to knock boots with is causing you to settle for the one with nothing to offer but a bad experience...chasing after the most intense climax you have ever had and wanting the next person to duplicate that feeling, or better yet, STALKING the one that you had the 'fabulous' experience with...refusing to trust your first mind when you get that feeling to leave a person alone or to remove yourself from the situation, but going ahead and doing it anyway because you were 'caught up' in the moment.

For some of us, this is a real existence and an everyday struggle to battle. It's like a crack head or an alcoholic who scrambles around for something or someone to give them a hit. You've seen many folks on the corner begging for money knowing that they are supporting some form of habit. But with Sexual Addiction, the begging is done differently - unless someone has chosen the route of prostitution to get that monkey off their back.

Most times, those of us who are going through an episode of wanting to become reckless tend to bask in stories of sexual adventures. We tend to set our sights on things that we know are unattainable in order to give us an 'excuse' to 'go out and run rampant'. We tend to start arguments for no apparent reason looking for that 'excuse'. We set ourselves up for failure in order to have that 'woe is me' or 'why does this always happen to me?' feeling. And then, we go out for the kill!!! Whether it is with one person or a thousand, we set out to squash the feelings of inadequacy, depression, loneliness, unworthiness, and all of the other adjectives used to describe someone with a low self image. We compromise integrity and our dignity in order to not experience whatever pain may be emerging.

There is an even darker side to all of this: the mental anguish one suffers. It's hard for those of us who deal with sexual addiction to overcome feelings of jealousy, rage, envy, denial, and rejection whenever someone we care about or wanted to be in a relationship or courtship with is having fun-filled sexual experiences and it's not us...or better yet, not *with* us!!!

I truly believe this is the hardest part of overcoming addiction: sex, though it is a learned behavior, is a NEED! Now arguably, some will say that sex is a strong want, and in a lot of instances, that's true. But once the body has been awakened to these sensations, it then requires the need for a release and if it is not done manually (you go out and get some), the body will do it automatically (you will have a wet dream).

For those who are in recovery, it's difficult to have to monitor your behavior in order not to go overboard into a reckless spiral with something so intimate and personal as sex. Whenever we are 'going through', it's hard to be completely happy for friends and associates who are getting their grove on and you can't or won't because of fear of relapsing. Jealousy kicks into high gear because the feeling is 'they can do something that I can't' or 'they don't want to be bothered with me so they reached out to a complete stranger instead' (this is when the person we're close to is an object of our desire). Envy is right behind jealousy because the feeling is 'it should have been me' and covetousness reigns supreme as we create a world of delusion and despair about something that has NOTHING to do with us! Rage follows directly behind that as we question 'why isn't it me?' and all of the fabricated answers only facilitate the feelings of despair and anguish.

This has put my relationships with my friends in jeopardy. Those who are my best friends are there for the long haul, but it does wear on them. Sometimes they, too, get to a point of wanting to break away from me. Once I get that feeling, THAT triggers another bout with despair, anguish, and abandonment. I thank God daily, hourly, and during every second for my best friends because they have shown me unconditional love, and if they can get through this with me, thenWE can do anything!!!

Oh yes!!! It is real! I try to control my demon by not talking about it or by eating huge amounts of chocolate, which is one of the many telltale signs that I am 'going through'. I encourage all of you who read this to examine your behavior closely and ask yourself if you fit any of the aforementioned characteristics, and mind you, that is not all of them. For more information, go to www.sarr.org or www.sexaddictionhelp.com.

I hope this sheds light on a taboo subject that most folks do not wish to talk about or acknowledge. It is my prayer that this sparks OPEN, HONEST DISCUSSION with everyone who is willing to face the truth that SEXUAL ADDITCTION EXISTS and IS REAL! TRUST ME, this journey is NO JOKE!!!

The GAY Steppin' Fletcher

In a world where acceptance and image is EVERYTHING, the depths and lengths that one will go through to gain understanding and validation from a mainstream population still amazes me. Many times, it's blatantly obvious that the mainstream population does not seem to care one way or the other if one is an active part of the continuum or not. Yet, oftentimes, we will nearly kill ourselves for their approval.

This statement holds true for the LGBT community in epidemic proportions and it's nearly been deemed a travesty against humanity. The LGBT community has oftentimes resorted to relying on their sensational shtick: overt ostentaciousness, colorful commentaries, flamboyant flair, quick quips, and joking gestures to provide mainstream society with the entertainment and fuel it needed to continue to ridicule and ostracize a community looking for love and a sense of belonging. These actions are no different from those taken by those who came before us...the Mr. Bojangles, the Amos and Andys, the Fat Girl/Guy in the smorgasbord line, etc.

The LGBT community has lost itself in the battle of integration and assimilation into mainstream culture. Realizing that the community is a subculture of a subculture, the LGBT community continues to lose grace points by succumbing to the pressure of needing to PERFORM for the masses and going into their 'GAY STEPPIN' FLETCHER' routine!!!

Instead of being themselves, the LGBT community becomes caricatures of the people they THINK they are and who they THINK the mainstream culture wants them to be!!! The lavish language and the frolicking finger snaps, in addition to the posh posture and the inviting innuendos, have all become classic routines by which our mainstream counterparts have insisted that we define ourselves.

The GAY STEPPIN' FLETCHER is to always be ready at the drop of a dime to provide entertainment and to shed enlightenment on who's gay and who's not to the masses. Should we REFUSE to participate, chaos ensues and problems develop...or even WORSE: WE ARE NO LONGER ACCEPTED by our peers or by our mainstream counterparts!!!

The GAY STEPPIN' FLETCHER is always supposed to accept being the brunt of all the jokes, mockeries, scandals, harassments, dehumanizing principles, and degrading humor without pause or challenge. IF WE DO CHALLENGE IT, then The GAY STEPPIN' FLETCHER is now a troublemaker and is too serious, always coming out of a bag, and needs to lighten up a little.

The GAY STEPPIN' FLETCHER is not supposed to be

so GAY that it hurts the image of OTHER GAY STEPPIN' FLETCHERS because then it creates internal pandemonium and upset and for those who don't subscribe to GAY STEPPIN' FLETCHER's beliefs. GAY STEPPIN' FLETCHER must now fight harder for normalcy and equity to be accepted into mainstream culture.

Does any of this sound familiar? Does anyone pay attention to history/herstory anymore? For those who feel that the LGBT community is not connected in any way to the Civil Rights Struggle, isn't this exactly how many Blacks felt about images of themselves on the silver screen and in publications? Wasn't this how their White counterparts perceived them to be? Isn't this a part of the struggle for equality and the edification of a people, a race, and a culture?

Now here's the sad part: many of us THINK and BELIEVE that The GAY STEPPIN' FLETCHER is just a NATURAL part of us!!! Many would contest this offering and stand on the belief that they are only being themselves and that NO ONE can tell them how to act or behave. I KNOW...I was one of them!!!

The GAY STEPPIN' FLETCHER only emerges when HETERO-ATTRACTIONALS are around!!! HAAAAAAAAAAAAAA!!! That's the thing right there (finger snap)...GAY STEPPIN' FLETCHER is the bridge to the world of HETERO-ATTRACTIONAL friendships and camaraderie. GAY STEPPIN'

FLETCHER is the litmus test for approval and courtship. GAY STEPPIN' FLETCHER is the MASK needed to shield the pain and hurt one may experience if rejected and scorned. And like most images, the time has come for GAY STEPPIN' FLETCHER to retire and rest!!! That image is no longer required to edify one's existence or to glorify the mainstream's distaste for a culture it doesn't understand! It is our BIRTHRIGHT to stand tall and BE who we are AUTHENTICALLY and not to be the FABRICATED versions of who we THOUGHT we ought to be!!!

Believe and understand this: if we are created in the IMAGE of the Divine CREATOR, then why would we allow ANYONE ELSE define whom we should be, what we should do, and how we should behave???

Relax, children…it's completely okay to be yourself, but know that you don't have to show them pepper if salt is on the table!!! Always know, if it feels like you are jumping through hoops to make and keep a friend, you MUST ask yourself: is it really WORTH IT???

Thank you, Mr. GAY STEPPIN' FLETCHER, for attempting to open doors - but it's not worth me losing my dignity, integrity, and self-worth to walk through them!!! I'd rather do it on my OWN MERIT!!!

Time for a Career Change

Lately I've been discussing the idea of what life could have been like if I had not made soooooooooooooo many bad decisions during my 'development' period. I wonder what would have happened if I'd proceeded on with the plans that I had set for myself and what life would be like if I had reached all of the goals I planned to accomplish by certain landmark ages. I recently celebrated my 39th birthday throughout the entire month of March, although the 4th is my b-day, and this time I have come into such an AWAKENING that I am bursting at the seams!!! For the first time in my life, I REALLY BELIEVE I CAN HAVE AND CAN DO ANYTHING I PUT MY MIND TO!!!

When I arose on March 5th, a NEWNESS in me was stirred and NOW I SEE what my mother and those whom I love and respect have been teaching me up until this point in my life!!! The ancestors have rained down on me and supplied me with DIVINE sight into what CAN BE because I AM THEIR vision for tomorrow. Just like our ancestors dreamed about what tomorrow would be like for us, I CAN SEE what the tomorrow will be like for my nieces, nephews, and one day, MY children.

You see, I was struggling with mistakes that I made

over the past 20-plus years of my life. I was struggling with the fact that I lead a lifestyle that is contrary to that of the norm, and in MOST cases, contrary to the people whom I kept company with!!! During the time that I was accepting that I am a GAY man, the emergence of 'The Diva' within me lead me to carry the torch for all of us who had to do battle with the mainstream and TAKE the necessary concessions REQUIRED to live and COEXIST with our hetero-attractional counterparts.

While defining my life as a GAY man…an African-American Gay Man who is overweight with above average intelligence and is not the most masculine, mind you, being GAY became my career choice. My mantra was: the best person for the job is not the man or the woman; it's the SISSY because the SISSY will get the job DONE with the Brawn of a Man and the Brain of a Woman. My trademark was the infamous right-handed finger snap, reminiscent of the STAX RECORDS logo. I learned all kinds of TRICKS, TRADE, and Tricks of the Trade to sustain my career. I've learned how to build equity in my GAY existence and how to be a mentor to the 'newbies' joining the company. I've been promoted from being a Newbie, to Queen, to Mother, to Queen Mother, to Mother of the HOUSE in a matter of 5 short years. I've received all kinds of awards and accolades for my performance. I've even created training manuals and presentations; I've represented the company in several endeavors with prominent people in prestigious places. I became an authority on 'company policy' and I have been sought after for advice, counsel, and care. I've been adored by those who have been in the company for much longer than I...

The sad thing about all of the time, effort, and energy put into this company is that a recessional depression came and destroyed all of the work I've so diligently designed and deliciously demonstrated. I did NOT receive all of the benefits that MOST OTHER COMPANIES afford such loyal employees. The retirement plan is astronomically atrocious; there is no 401(k), stock option, or health benefits package. The other company members inject a very special brand of 'HATER-ADE' and are not accepting of the gifts and talents that one has to offer.

For all the work and tireless commitment I've given to my GAY career I, like many others, have NOTHING TO SHOW FOR IT but memories, misfortunes, and a complete WAREHOUSE full of torch songs that remind me of what it means to be 'utterly FABULOUS' and 'sexually liberated'...

Now even though I carry my card well and I stand by my honors and my credentials...NOR am I ready to retire...I've had to come to the conclusion that LIFE IS MORE THAN BEING GAY!!!

I've spent so much time encouraging, nurturing, and expanding my GAY skills that I have forgotten to broaden ALL my LIFE skills. I've been so busy concentrating on ONE facet of my career that I did not realize that a plethora of talent and skills lie within the realms of my being, my TRUE essence!

After 20-plus years of clubs, misunderstandings, and trade and cat fights, I began to see that something was not necessarily right.

After 20-plus years of going to clubs and seeing the SAME people, sitting on the SAME bar stools, drinking the SAME cocktails, arguing about the SAME things, fighting the SAME people, talking about and/or not speaking to the SAME people (especially if they have made transition), I discovered that I have outgrown my career and I knew it was time to do something about it.

After 20-plus years of looking at a dead end job as a career, I've finally learned:

IT'S TIME FOR A CAREER CHANGE!!!

The time has come for me to shake things up a bit, remove my comfort shackles, and experience LIFE! The time has come for me to step in to LIVING and out of SURVIVAL mode!

This career change means that I have the opportunity to embrace NEW skills and incorporate what I've learned from the OLD job into the new one; I'm learning how to be an ASSET to ME and the new job! It means that I can make mistakes and LEARN from them and not be such the professional at covering them up because NO ONE would care anyway!

Ms. Thing...it's Time for a Career Change!!!

This career change means NEW people and a NEW class of folk that can experience what I have to offer and I can touch MORE lives and THEY can touch mine. This career change means that I have a new focus, new goals, and that I can put those things I placed on the back burner on the front burner because I was blinded by my own inadequacies and superficiality. This career change means that I can come from behind the wall of shame, guilt, hurt, and scorn and MOVE FORWARD rather than stay still in a spot I've called home - but it was really a mask for an EXCUSE!

Yes, Ms. Honey...it's Time for a Career Change!

This career change means that I must apply myself with the same tenacity, fervor, and determination used to sustain my former career to blossom into the rose I've been telling everyone I am; but I have only allowed the stem and the thorns to overshadow my beauty and delicate, yet resilient nature. This career change means that I give myself permission to accept new facets of ME without ridicule or scorn. It means that I can embrace MY totality…the Masculine and Feminine…the Mother and Big DADDY. It means that I don't need to be bewitched by a bevy of bars and brothels; instead I can sustain myself in the sweet surrender of Success and Sophistication! It means that I no longer have to provide the masses with my rendition of the Gay Steppin' Fletcher and subject myself to being dehumanized and ostracized simply because the mainstream insists on labeling me!!! This career change means that I am ME and Gay is just a piece of the puzzle!

I welcome new challenges, new horizons, new hopes, and new dreams as I embrace this wonderful endeavor of self-discovery and enlightenment!!! Now I may be a little older and a little set in some of my ways, BUT I KNOW a good thing when I see and feel it!!! This career change is moving me in the right direction!!! I encourage you to join me on this journey and let's show each other our REAL Fabulousness and RECEIVE all that the Creator has for us WITHOUT limiting ourselves to the mundane!!!

Oh yes, my darling...it's Time for a CAREER CHANGE!

What Do I Want From a MAN?

This question was asked in an online discussion group and I would like to share my thoughts on the subject. For those of you who are of the LGBT community, particularly those who identify as MSMs (Men who have Sex with Men), you will feel my plight. For my heterosexual family, my sistahs will understand me completely. My bruthas, I would like for you to carefully scrutinize what I am saying and pull from it what you need to in order to enhance your relationships with your lady friends, wives, potential girlfriends, etc.

This is created to encourage dialogue, so I invite ALL who read this to let your voice be heard and respond as you feel. I welcome ALL points of view!!!

What do I want from a MAN?

This is a really good question!!! Many of us DON'T KNOW HOW TO ANSWER THAT BECAUSE WE HAVE BEEN CONDITIONED TO...

'BE MEN AND DO WHAT MEN DO'...

regardless of how feminine one may be. We have allowed society to dictate to us WHAT OUR ROLE IS

TO BE and HOW WE MUST ACT! Many of us do not know HOW TO LOVE OR BE LOVED because SEX has always been the avenue to love!!! Heartbreak is the road that leads to a life of joyless, disconnecting carnal pleasures which leads to misery, strife, and hopelessness!!! Furthermore, it's sad because many of us don't believe that we DESERVE anything more than a roll in the hay with a mindless stranger!!!

I am now in a space where I can appreciate and accept that I want INTIMACY and COURTSHIP!!! For those who read my profiles on bear411 and wherever else I may place one, that's what I now deem my creed!!!

For those who don't understand...first off, you may NOT be someone that I would consider to have any kind of serious potential. You will mainly be used for my carnal pleasures ONLY.

INTIMACY: This does not mean SEX ONLY!!! This means being able to have decent, wholesome conversations in which we learn one another and gain insight into EACH OTHER and WHO THE OTHER PERSON IS!!! This is the time where I get to understand what makes you tick and what ticks you off!!! This is the time where I can appreciate your likes and dislikes and determine if I can add you to my life AND if my likes and dislikes are compatible with yours!!! This is the time where I can find joy holding hands while watching television or reading a book and I STILL want you in my presence or space!!! This is the time where WE CREATE THE WORLD WE WANT TO LIVE IN...and not focus on just fucking!!!

COURTSHIP: This is the space where we learn HOW TO TREAT ONE ANOTHER!!! This is the space where WE LEARN how to make one another smile and how to be the sunshine of one's day!!! This is the space where foreplay is created!! NOW GET THIS: FOREPLAY MEANS THAT YOU ARE MAKING LOVE TO MY MIND, NOT MY LOINS!!! THIS IS THE SPACE WHERE WE LEARN TO FALL IN LOVE WITH ONE ANOTHER, NOT BECAUSE THE DICK OR THE ASS IS GOOD, BUT BECAUSE OF HOW WE TREAT AND RESPECT EACH OTHER!!! It is in this space where one's actions created the yearning and desire to want to keep YOU as a partner and not as some notch on the bedpost!!! It is in this space where fantasy and dreams come true for the two of us!!! It is in this space where the spiritual and the physical aspects of love can connect and blossom ONLY IF YOU ARE TRUE with EACH OTHER!!!ß

I am NOT LOOKING for COMPLETION...I am looking for AFFIRMATION!

To look for COMPLETION implies that you are not whole...that you are missing something vital, that you cannot function without it, and you will do anything to make sure you get it!!! This means that you are willing to sacrifice your truth and happiness and you will ignore your joy for the sake of being in a relationship.

To seek AFFIRMATION implies that I am who and what I am and whoever is blessed to take my hand and stand by my side acknowledges and appreciates ME for ME…NOT the 'ME' they want me to be!!! This is not to change ME or them, but it means to walk in the TRUTH of who we are as individuals first, which brings spotlights our union!!!

That's what I want in a man: a person who understands and that is waiting for me to get in alignment with MY TRUTH so that HE can manifest in my life…for my life!!!

Why I 'CHOSE' to be Gay

This question was asked in an online discussion group I belong to. I was riveted to respond because of my passion on this subject. I am welcoming all who read this to respond because it creates the dialogue needed to surpass the ignorance and hypocrisy that the LGBT is faced with on a continuous basis. Let me hear what YOU think and feel!!!

Why I CHOSE to be GAY?

I am COMPELLED to weigh in on this topic!!!

I want the world to FIRMLY understand that none of us CHOSE to BE gay...we JUST ARE!!! If there was a CHOICE, it was to finally live in the truth of it!!! Because society wants the world to believe that being gay is THE WORST SIN IN LIFE, many of us had to shelter those feelings and become a LIE unto ourselves by living up to what we thought our parents, bosses, friends, etc. thought we should be!!! Proving our masculinity and normality was always on the forefront of our existence!!!

It's even worse if you happen to have been a feminine child like myself!!! EVERYTHING I did was WRONG and I had to fight all my life (I feel like Sofia from The Color Purple) to BE ME!!!

As for SEX...the body is DESIGNED to receive pleasure!!! Once that door is opened, the body reacts to what then becomes a need. That's why children are confused when they are violated because that door is opened much too soon. I was 'turned out' by my FEMALE babysitter!!! I learned how to do EVERYTHING with a Va-Jay-Jay, except have a baby; that would have made my father PROUD that his firstborn was just like him...YET I am NOT HETEROSEXUAL!!! The idea that children are 'turned out' has to be examined because children only act out what they believe is right and 'feels good', which then results in them 'Choosing to be GAY'. For those of us who did not have that kind of horror to contend with, we had to deal with the night sweats and the hurtful yearning to be true to what our bodies were saying, but we had to DENY IT, because something was wrong with us or we were possessed with the DEVIL!!!

The day when we DECIDED to end that HELL was 'THE CHOICE' to be GAY!!! The choice to be FREE of the torture, shame, and ridicule that WE PUT ON OURSELVES!!!

What we did not CHOOSE was to be ostracized, dehumanized, disenfranchised, and categorized as pedophiles, dregs of society, and disease-spreading, unnatural, hell-bound whoremongers!!! In this society, that's what being GAY means...and THAT is something that NO ONE CHOOSES!!!

I AM Gay...simply because I AM - not because I
CHOSE to BE!!!

Epilogue

As I continue along this journey called LIFE, I am confidently certain that I will receive more epiphanies and Awakening Moments that will propel me into MY future. It is my hope that this offering will promote dialogue in your home and amongst your family and friends. Please share those things that you feel strongly about, whether or not you agree with what has been presented. Remember, these are MY epiphanies and if there is anything here that brings you peace and comfort, please share. If there is anything here that brings you pause or you disagree with, PLEASE SHARE. This is what these offerings are about; SHARING. Perhaps, after reading this, you have your OWN epiphanies and Awakenings that will catapult you into your AUTHENTICITY.

Thank you for your time and your kindness for reading.

NOTES